ENEMY LUCK

NICHOLAS LAUGHLIN

ENEMY LUCK

[a notebook]

PEEPAL TREE

First published in Great Britain in 2019
Peepal Tree Press Ltd
17 King's Avenue
Leeds LS6 1QS
UK

ISBN 13: 978184524393

Supported using public funding by
ARTS COUNCIL
ENGLAND

Sending love to my friends and foes
I suppose

CONTENTS

*

**

***

For I am not without authority in my jeopardy
—— *Christopher Smart*

*

ENEMY MEDICINE

Strangest things happen.
One morning you drink mercury instead of tea.
The doctors never get it right.

ENEMY FAVOURS

By day I sweat black honey.
Nightly I drown my sons
in the palm of my hand.

In a house of dead paper,
a question of turpentine:
why not burn everything there is to burn?

I can write my own damn reasons.
You can break your own damn laws.
My hates are no odds to me.

A bed is a kitchen where nothing burns.
I myself am still more bread
than meat.

There's no pleasing tomorrow,
no hoper than this,
no iffer after.

Enemy favours are their own reward.
There should be saints by now.

> *Witnessed*   Dr. August
>   Dr. Ace

ENEMY MATH

I understand the terms:

Day minus day,
weather into weather
into weather.

Now or nerver,
present tense,
subtraction trick.

You bruise a grammar before it bruises you.

I do remember how it goes:
chew the question till it tastes
like thank-you.
– Then it goes down.

Safe and out and neither and both
and safe and both
and neither.

Enemy answers keep me up all night,
and sleep is the reward of sleep,

unless it is sleeping with others.

ENEMY MISTAKES

Before these days there were other days
and before those there were days.

Behind the visible stars
are only invisible stars.

Errors are not accidents.

I count these days like buttons on an enemy shirt.

Imagine, I was born as myself,
irrevocable, no warning.

Even we who remember the future
are doomed to repeat it, at the incredible rate
of one second per second.

Do I look like a man with nothing to hide?
I am not that kind of mammal.   [anymore]

Not everything I finish must I start.

We moved around a lot and my

enemy. He always told me

His call letters were

UNCLE OBO HOW.

the naming do all the work

I'd go back right away."

work on the chemistry

a [spoiler] the whole time.

I WAS THE BOY HERO

Foreign words are best.
The less you know,
the less mistaken.

Somewhere it is always the wrong weather.
Is it the same year where you are?
Or continent.

The wrong wind takes my words away,
another wrong wind gives them back.
There is no schedule for rain.

I use only words I speak to myself.
Did I tell you I lived for you often before
without knowing it?

No one here is waiting for this news.
Is the place where you are now
the wrong place too?

THE STRANGER

We are joking and laughing as we return to my friend's house, but when we step inside we fall silent: the house is ransacked, chairs turned over, books pulled off their shelves, papers and small objects scattered across the floor. We begin to argue but almost at once we realise there has been an intruder, then some barely audible shuffle or sigh reveals the truth: the intruder is still here.

I cross the room, pause, fling open a door. There, standing in the dark, and now frowning at us, is the intruder. There are two of us, my friend and I, we outnumber him, so I grab the intruder by the arm and pull him roughly into the room where we can punish him. But the intruder seems confused. You don't remember? he asks. I am the stranger from Les Deux Renards. And right away we recognise him, though a moment ago he was unknown to us. He is the stranger we met not an hour before, the young man we found sitting at our restaurant table, who we parted from with compliments and regrets. But why is he here?

The stranger pulls from his pocket a piece of paper patterned in red and yellow, unfolds it for us: it is a map to my friend's house and a letter inviting a visit, its sentences written in a beautiful old-fashioned hand, and though we don't recall giving it to the stranger, we don't doubt it is genuine.

So there is a reasonable explanation for everything, there is no trouble anymore, and I'm sorry I grabbed the young man's arm so roughly. He nods at my stammered apology, he turns to leave, and now I am anxious, realising I don't know his name or where to find him, uncertain how I will meet him again.

THE UNCLE

When the time comes to pack the last of my things, I open the drawer of a desk and discover its contents belong to my companion, who has already departed. The drawer is full of money: coins and small bills, tied into little packets and bundles, each labelled with a slip of paper. And each label records some kind of minor offence – fibs, irritations, gaucheries: so my companion has been "fining" himself for these infractions, dozens of them, unknown to me, for months. The little packets of coins with their paper slips are arranged in neat rows inside the drawer, which until now I have never thought to open.

I turn at the creak of the door. A middle-aged man is standing there, half-smiling. I've never seen him before. He is my companion's "uncle," he says, but I don't believe him, and he says he has come to take away the things my companion left behind – the little packets of coins. He reaches for the open drawer and I grab his wrist. This is a dangerous man, I somehow know, but I must not let him steal my companion's modest treasury, his collection of modest sins. I tell the man I don't believe his claim, don't believe he has any right. His smile broadens. I argue. I will report him, I say, to the authorities, though I know there is no authority to intervene. He doesn't raise his voice, his tone is even and sinister. I call him *sir*, repeatedly, but really to show my hostility.

If I don't act boldly now, I know, all will be lost. With no warning I push the man out of the room, catching him by surprise, I slam the door, turn the key, and I hurriedly look for a bag big enough to carry away the entire drawer and its contents, because if I don't steal it this man will, and soon he will return, it will be too late.

LETTER FROM THE ISLE OF MAN

You see this name above, take not
affright, my ink is innocent,
my only spelling now is words.

Did not breathe against the world
that weighs a thousand names on me,
and threats are knotted in my hair.

Three times up and down the street,
bell and unlit candle, bare
of feet, and every guilt I drank.

Gave my promise, do not speak,
cowled in ivy, fast and wake,
wait these famous days to end.

But now am hungry as an owl
waiting for its small prey to get born.

Michael Drayton, Elinor Cobham to Duke Humphrey

LEUCADIANS

It was the custom long ago, on the feast of Apollo, to catch the first stranger and drag him along to Lovers' Leap. Then throw him off the long white cliff: but first they would rig him with homemade wings and fans and sails, and garland him with birds, to ease his fall. Down below the fishermen would gather their boats and nets, waiting to scoop the fallen stranger out of the waves, so often he would not drown. Then they would race him out to sea, the boats laden with the stranger's gear and his clothes, his household charms, his kitchen pans, his chequebooks, whatever half-torn photos he still possessed, race him out of sight of land, thanking the stranger for his courage and his travels and his noble plight.

Strabo, Geography, *X.2.9*

MORALITÉ

A loaf of bread wrapped in a shirt of feathers
is not a new bird.

No hay las enfermedades que en otras tierras, y si hay malos humores, el calor los consume, y así dicen que no son menester allí médicos.

— *Juan de Torquemada*

**

SOME INCIDENTS

Embarcation. – Fellow-passengers. – A gale at sea. – Ornithological specimens. – Principle of the game. – Passion for gambling. – Serious accidents. – A noble beast. – Effects on moral character. – A concert, and its arrangements. – Fête of Todos Santos. – An old friend. – Presentation to the Governor. – A citizen of the world.

Ruined cities of America. – A chapter of contingencies. – Give up this business. – A little hero. – Instability of fame. – An accident. – Unpromising appearances. – How to make a fire. – Instance of perseverance. – Perplexities. – Indian mode of boiling eggs. – A breach made in the wall. – Prints of a red hand. – Loss of antiquities by the burning of Mr. Catherwood's Panorama.

Execrable roads. – Fête of Santiago. – Miracles. – Fireworks. – Threading a labyrinth. – An alarm. – An abrupt termination. – Labyrinth not subterraneous. – News from home. – A Campo Santo. – Means by which the city was supplied with water. – Great exertions. – A bitter disappointment. – Arrival of Dr. Cabot, ill with fever.

Gloomy prospects. – Archives of the convent. – Another ruined city. – A beautiful vase. – These cities not built by descendants of Egyptians. – Their antiquity not very great. – The seybo tree. – House of the Birds. – House of the Dwarf. – Tasteful arrangement of ornaments. – Newyear's Day. – Municipal elections. – The democratic principle. – Uses of the well.

A plurality of Saints. – How to put a Saint under patronage. – A procession. – Fireworks. – Rankness of tropical vegetation. – A solitary arch. – Scarcity of water. – The Casa Cerrada. – Want of interest manifested by the Indians in regards to these ruins. – Hornet's nest. – Young vulture. – Continued scarcity of water. – Delicate manner of doing a service. – Fanciful scene.

30

A crisis in money matters. – Mingling of old things with new. – Effects of a good breakfast. – Costumes. – Dance of the Toros. – Love in a phrensy. – A storm. – Dispersal of the spectators. – A few words about the padres. – Rain. – Daguerreotyping. – Paved road. – Imposing gateway. – An inhospitable host.

Precipitous descents. – Rude ladders. – Great number of ladders. – Seven basins in all. – Want of philosophical instruments. – Annoyance from fleas. – Moonlight scene. – Love of the marvellous. – Oppressive attentions. – Lazy escort. – Deplorable condition of the country in regard to medical aid. – Great idol of the figure of a horse. – Broken by the monks, who in consequence are obliged to leave the island. – From the church to the gaming-table.

Journey resumed. – An effort in the Maya language. – Grove of orange trees. – Garrapatas. – Black ants. – A bloodless revolution. – Curiosity of the people. – Historical notice. – Ambassadors murdered. – Crowd of loungers. – Mischievous boys. – Buying a wardrobe. – Failure of the corn crop. – Hieroglyphics.

Staircase, having on each side entwined serpents. – Extraordinary edifice, to which the name gymnasium or tennis-court is given. – Procession of tigers. – Gamecocks. – Fate of Molas the Pirate. – Plans deranged. – Arrival at the port. – Different kinds of turtle. – Sharks. – Moschetoes. – Present state of the island. – Overgrown with trees. – These buildings probably the towers seen by the Spaniards. – Vanity of human expectations.

Opinion of the old Spanish writers. – An iron-bound coast. – Fearful apprehensions. – A man overboard. – Sudden change of feeling. – Ibises. – The grave of Lafitte – Flamingoes and spoonbills. – Giraffes. – Colossal ornaments in stucco. – The great question of the Revolution undecided. – Parting with friends. – A ludicrous adventure. – A legend.

I AM A POEM ABOUT THE ANTS

Also the ants here are different,
they make nests high in the trees,
adorn them with flowers, adorn them with small birds
snared in webs of silk, iridescent and anxious,
the ants are fervent collectors of honey,
they keep their treasury high in the trees,
a fortune in honey,
so when it rains, the rain falls golden and sweet,
and the hummingbirds take refuge in their burrows.
Only the spiders dare parley with the ants.
Do not believe there is sugar in the sky.

I AM A MAP OF THE SAVANNAHS

A black snake thirsty for salt
fell asleep with a dream of the sea.
A red snake hungry for quartz,
we have not seen its head for a thousand years.

Never call me mighty. Never call me vast.
I am the lord's handkerchief.
I am four claws in the mud,
I am four weeping scars, named and remembered.

The lord sleeps long in the river,
his hair grows a thousand miles long,
swift as a season, shining in the mud,
a thousand razors dreaming of gold.

Why should a mountain be more patient than a god?
Lord of a vulture's voice.

The lord returns on a tide of dust,
thirst like a navy of spiders, his stride is their north.
The lord will know his own name when he comes,
its vowels new as bruises,
a mouthful of permanent salt.

The lord has nothing to say.
His census is trapped in a thousand stones.
A thousand times the rivers climb and fall,
his citizens are not afraid to drown.

PERSONAL NAMES FOR CLAN JAGUAR

[jaguar] heard close at night
[jaguar] in my sleep
[jaguar] confides in no one
omen-eyed [jaguar]

[jaguar] who steps in man's footprint
[jaguar] leaving handsome tracks
[jaguar] dainty fisher
[jaguar] not yet seen by a man's eyes

[jaguar] dives deeper than a river
[jaguar] does not believe in the sea
soft-breathing [jaguar], rustles no leaves
[jaguar] with a coat of new flowers

[jaguar] crowned with arrows
[jaguar] ten to one
[jaguar] has never been tempted to break the rules
[jaguar] or hummingbird

first-time [jaguar], not yet reborn
[jaguar] with a coat of hot coals
[jaguar] knows more than one edition of hunger
[jaguar] pauses: air turns to glass

[jaguar] of a dream that may be interpreted
[jaguar] of a dream no one has interpreted
[jaguar] in the silence of a bell
[jaguar] who is not yet dangerous, but soon

I AM A DREAM OF RIVERS

Inevitably, he began to dream of rivers, or perhaps of a single river, unimaginably long, its source as impossible as its mouth, ceaselessly changing, ceaselessly the same, its black waters concealing impossible depths. He dreamt of a house on the bank of this river, a wooden house with open sides, among trees, the damp wood of the house no less alive than the wood of the trees, the wind tumbling through the branches of the trees the same wind that tumbled through the house, and the rush of the wind making the same sound as the black water rushing over the rocks of the river. For the house was close enough to the rapids for the river's spray to drench its posts and walls; but also – for such is the unstable topography of dreams – the house was on a great height overlooking the river, so high that the river's course was spread out below as on a map, a line of black or of gold traced through the green fog of the forest, black or gold, depending on the angle of the sun. And at this height the winds were warm and seemed tinged with pink and gold, but lower down, among the trees, where the wind gushed along the course of the river, the rays of the sun did not reach, it was always dark and damp and chilly in the permanent weather of this dream. It was always dusk, never day, and in the dark beneath the trees, along the forest floor muffled with dead leaves, it was always silent but for the sounds of the wind and the river, no birds called, no insects hummed, and the dark air was heavy with the weight of that silence.

From this house on the height above the river he would plan his journey, unfurling old maps that sometimes matched the river he could see far below. He did not know his destination, but he knew it lay somewhere along the river, further than the maps showed; he did not know when the journey would start, but he knew it would be soon, and his rucksack lay on the wooden floor beside him, half open, clothes and small gear spilling out onto the floor. He had many visitors in this house, perhaps, because he could hear their voices, perhaps from another room, though it sometimes seemed the voices came from the trees, people chatting and laughing and never calling his name; but he was also a stranger in this house, he did not know what had brought him here, could not remember finding his way, and though he searched and searched his maps, turning them round and round on the table in the fading light, his face inches from the old, creased paper, his maps never told him where he had come from, and all they showed was the river, a long, meandering, spiralling line of black or of gold, the names of its islands and banks and tributaries unfamiliar and unhelpful, its many channels crossing and weaving so that it was not clear if it was one river or many, and the river of his maps only sometimes matched the river he could see outside, far below, and he did not know where the maps had come from. And though night never fell, night was always about to fall, it was always the moment just before he knew dusk had turned into night, and then in the wooden house with open sides on the bank of the river, so close that the spray from the rapids drenched the posts and walls of the house, he would shiver and listen to the rushing water falling on the rocks like knives, and wonder if it would rain that night, and, if it rained, how high the river would rise.

Sometimes this dream turned into the dream of nothing, which was an older dream, perhaps the first dream. It was a dream of falling asleep, of the moment between waking and sleeping when the dreamer must let go of things, of even the thought of sleep. Except he felt something in his arms, his arms were wrapped around something, something invisible without form or weight, a nothing, except he felt it in his arms and he tried to hold it fast, but the nothing in his arms seemed to grow bigger and bigger without ever changing, and he tried to hold it fast and stop it from growing, but because it had no form or weight it was unstoppable, and could not even be held, and then he realised he was sinking, but through a vast space so dark and empty he barely knew he was sinking, as if he were sinking through the very nothing he was trying to hold fast in his arms.

He wanted to let go, to stop trying to hold this nothing. Later he would know he did stop, because he did finally fall asleep, but he never knew how, and each time he had this dream he believed this was the time it would not end.

This was the oldest dream and the worst one, because it was really a dream of never sleeping and never waking. It was a dream of always being in the dream itself, in the impossible space between waking and sleeping, of always sinking and always trying to hold fast in his arms the nothing that could not be held or stopped. As a child, he had this dream nearly every night, and then for many years it had gone. Now the dream came back.

The secret plan of gravity is no secret, no plan.

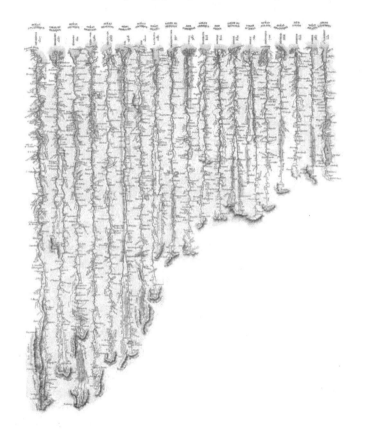

COUSIN HERMES

Hard Luck

You learn the hardest way
(last night in the red hotel,
the third key, the fourth lock,
the fifth pocket – if he's French,
I'm the archbishop; heads the needle,
tails the ice, "these are not the droids
you're looking for"; define a "one man job";
don't keep the doctor waiting,
don't wake the doctor up):
never let Cousin Hermes deal the cards.

Hermes the Cheat

Did you love it and love it and love it?
– Cousin Hermes at the door,
both hands empty,
both hands full,

both hands behind his back.

Like a blind man with a mirror in his pocket,
I thought the chance was mine –
I almost said, to lose.
I meant, to refuse.

Promises are promises,
gods are still gods,
there are fourteen ways (at least) to ask a question,
fourteen answers, most of them wrong,
most of all *Yes*.

Bad Boys vs. Good Boys

Bad boys vs. good boys is Cousin Hermes' game.
Little god of a torn shirt and cut lip
and quarter yes and half a maybe.

The first trick is the oxygen trick.
The milk trick is a better trick
than the chlorophyll trick, according to the rules.

But he likes the kerosene trick.
He likes it too much.
(Trick is cousin to mistake.)

Meanwhile I am always one fib behind,
three mercies. This is the handcuff trick,
extra points to bruise,

and Cousin Hermes was born to twist my tongue,
born to win.
So: *Open your mouth. We're cousins.*

[honey is not the only drop that stains]

His Nicknames

Which he mostly gave himself.
Boss of mirrors.
Boss of spies.
Author of the great Olympian novel.
Boss of keys.
Lord of tongues.
Lord of dirty jokes.
Hermes who leaves no footprints.
Hermes who needs no thanks.
Hermes the laughing orphan.
God of the lost and found.
Hermes who always wins at Scrabble.
Hermes who never needs to tell a fib,
since *Only truth can come out of this pretty mouth*.
Hermes, lord of alibis.
Loanshark to your dreams.
Maestro for the bees.
Hermes the frequent flyer.
Hermes, permanent King of the Bands.
Best friend Hermes.
Sir Sumo Hence.
Cousin of them all.
Television star, wins all the quiz shows,
wrote all the scripts.
One-man championship of Chinese Whispers.
Hermes hello-stranger.
Hermes who knows what to do with crybabies.
Hermes the danger-man.
Hermes who wrote the codes.
God of the sure thing.
Alias Johnny Otro.
Hermes who never needs to check the map.
Mr. Too Smart to Be an Angel.

All the Way Down

Cousin Hermes on an empty stomach,
drinking what he calls *You call that fire?*
I'll give you something to burn.
All the way down, in hero gulps.
I spill one glass for every glass I swallow
and bite one finger
for every missing thumb.
For every tongue / there is a salty drop
of cousin.
– On what it feels like this time,
don't waste a name.
If he never says *please*
he sometimes says *sorry*.

My Turn

This time we were playing the password game
and every guess was wrong.
Pigeon. *No*. Pratfall. *No*. Promise. *Time to pay*.

The price is one needle at a time,
one fingertip. One liver. O my elbow,
you will never be the same.

But Cousin Hermes only plays it fair.
I told you it wouldn't leave a scar.

What is the name of the animal they drown in molasses?

Round two. Mortal rules.
                                    Paris. *No*.

Sweet Talk

It is nothing like making jam,
never mind it's red
and sticky.

Think of it as vitamins,
gods don't have germs.

Nonsuch

I learned all my jokes from Cousin Hermes —
god of punchlines, after all —
even if they're funnier in Greek. (He always says.)

Of course you know I invented the alphabet too,
I'm not sure this is true, but where do I look it up?
Also postage stamps
and the magnetic compass
and the arts of swimming
and tossing coins.
Ask my brothers.

He says he remembers before there were enough spare words
    to donate lies.

Once I wrote a language with no rhymes,
for fun, and another one where every word rhymes.
Neither any good for poems, oddly.

It doesn't mean what you think it means
when I say I was born yesterday.

By the way, there is no such thing as a lucky poem.
I should know.

Cousin Degrees

Once removed,
twice the man,
thrice jarmed,
fourtholemew.
Eightful,
nined to the power of ten,
dozenless.
Love—nil.
Half the odds for two red jacks,
one named Cousin, one named Mr. Sicks.

Gods Are Still Gods

An hour of trouble
is worth three of the cousin.

[traditional proverb]

Cousin Hermes in Sebastian drag,
reading the lives of the saints:
an epic of nets, of snares, of nooses,
hooks, awls, screws, elastic cables,
beaks, briars, saws, electric wires,
matches and pliers.

"The archers shot at him till he was as full of arrows
as an urchin is full of pricks."

Once they tried to burn me for a heathen,
look how that turned out,
braggish in his noonday tan
and rosy as a loaf.
He calls it his summer plumage.

They have modern tastes
but gods are still gods.
Does anyone really prefer vanilla?

All Night Long

Meanwhile I am just another sleeping animal / to Cousin Hermes.
Gods don't need sleep.

So the whole mortal night with no one to blame,
no generals to bribe, no wives to fame,
Cousin Hermes paces every empty room,
overturning cups, cracking mirrors,
rearranging pages in my books,
devising little daylight ransoms.

So if I dream only traitors' dreams
that's his fault too,

Hermes, little god of being famous,

his tongue in the quaint of every knot,

his green ink on every screenplay.

Happy Birthday

Sometimes Cousin Hermes makes me blush.
All his little red-hot copper tips.

Ask me to show you my tattoo.
Imagine it took literally 2,500 years
under the sea.   [mortal years]

Gods don't rust,
gods don't drown,
gods hold their breath until they need it.

Don't act like you've never seen a naked god,
yawning, *You've read the classics.*   [in translation]

A god to his ears
and an angel to his nipples
and all cousin.

Teeth the most gleaming set of dice,
and they roll every wrong number.

Cousin Proverb

A bird in the hand
is already meat.

[line for an ostracon perhaps]

Ultra aequinoxialem non peccati.
—— *Caspar Barlaeus*

****

TO THE READER OF THESE ACCOUNTS

Reader, consider these accounts with indulgence; the country is very far away, few of our kind have travelled there, and even those few have seen only scattered parts, some of their stories came at second-hand, they had no choice but to travel in haste, and besides in the company of an army. It is no surprise their accounts so often disagree, though each one claims he saw these events and objects and marvels with his own eyes. Some of these writers were scholars, some were soldiers, some were spies; and when such intrepid men cannot agree among themselves, what are we to think who are sensible enough to remain at home?

Strabo, Geography, *XV. 1.2*

THEIR APPREHENSIONS WERE GREATER
THAN THE DANGER

What frightened the soldiers most was the magnitude of whales,
the commotion of their hundreds in the sea,
their blowing and groaning, the darkness of the night,
their own ships were invisible.
But *These are merely animals,* the pilots knew,
Drive them away with the sound of trumpets.
So the general rammed the fleet into the hills of the sea
with an emergency of trumpets,
and the whales dove and rose again
and dove and rose again, like the beginning of a war,
but soon they dove and did not rise.

The passage across the mouth of the Persian Gulf
takes no more than a day.

Strabo, Geography, *XV.2.12*

THIS IS WHAT HAS BEEN SAID
ON THE SUBJECT OF RAINS

In India there are winter and summer rains,
so a winter and a summer sowing,
and twice a year the land bears fruits and grains.
Both rains and rivers are warmed by the sun,
so the roots of plants possess a sweetness
which other lands call ripening.
The reeds yield honey, although there are no bees,
and here is a tree whose fruit yields honey if cooked
but eaten fresh causes intoxication.
For the same reason, some trees grow kernels of wool instead of flowers.
But other authors also say there is no wine in India,
hence no musical instruments save drums
and tambourines.

It is known that the waters of the Nile boil with half the heat
of the waters of India,
but the Indian rivers, pouring through vaster plains
and delayed in one hot climate,
are more nutritious than the waters of the Nile.
Hence the rivers of India yield larger porpoises
and in greater number.
So do not believe all nations are the same distance from the sun.

We speak of the rivers deserving notice.
We are ignorant of the rest.

Strabo, Geography, *XV. 1. 20–26*

ALSO, IT IS PROBABLE THERE ARE EARTHQUAKES

The rivers of India breed the same creatures as the rivers of Egypt,
save the hippopotamus;

foreign cattle which drink at the rivers of India
turn the same colour as the native herds;

and the creatures which are tame in our country are wild in theirs;

there are monkeys the size of dogs;
dogs with the disposition of tigers;
scorpions and serpents with wings;
ebony grows there
and yellowish pebbles that taste sweeter than figs;

there is a river on which nothing can float,
its vapours so rare that not even birds can fly across its course;

but that is a matter of physics.

Strabo, Geography, *XV. 1. 13,24,38,56*

SOMETIMES THE HISTORIANS AGREE

The Indians worship Zeus the god of rain, also the River Ganges and their local gods;

when the king washes his hair, it is a great holiday, with feasts and presents, and every man tries to outdo his neighbours;

the winged ants of India are known to mine gold, and like the rivers of Spain, the rivers of India bring gold from the hills;

at every festival, elephants lead the parade, necklaced and braceleted in gold and silver, also there are chariots drawn by horses and oxen, men dressed in gold and bearing bowls and chalices of gold, tables of gold, chairs of gold, face-basins of copper, set with emeralds and beryls and Indian rubies, shirts and capes of gold woven and embroidered, tame panthers and lions, buffalo decked in gold, tame birds, wild birds, all singing!

Oh, Cleitarchus says there are gold-wheeled carriages bearing entire trees with giant leaves, hung with gold cages and a multitude of tame birds, all singing, the bird called the orion sings the sweetest note and the bird called the catreus has the most splendid plumage, almost like a peacock, but let Cleitarchus tell you the rest.

This is the sort of interesting information you can get from the historians.

Strabo, Geography, *XV. 1.69*

THERE ARE OTHER ISLANDS BETWEEN THIS AND INDIA

Taprobane is said to breed elephants.
An island 5,000 stadia across, it is not known whether of length or breadth.
Seven days' sail from the southerly part of India,
in the direction of Ethiopia,
a dangerous voyage in double-prowed ships without holds or keels.
And thereabouts in the sea are animals as huge as whales
but resembling horses and camels and oxen.
It is a relief to learn of a country
of which one needs no opinion.

Strabo, Geography, *XV. 1. 14—15*

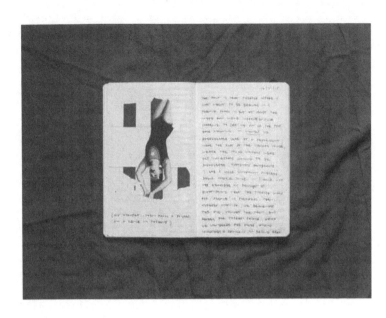

THE LETTER WAS WRITTEN IN GREEK
UPON A SKIN

Only three of the ambassadors from India survived the journey: let
that prove the distance.

"I saw them near Antioch, on their way to meet Caesar in Athens.
They came from King Porus, who called himself king of six hundred kings.
Eight naked servants, perfumed with roses, set out their royal gifts:
a hermes born without arms,
a serpent ten cubits long,
a river turtle three cubits wide,
a partridge bigger than a vulture.

"Later, one of these ambassadors burned himself at Athens,
a custom of the Indians.
After such a delicious life, he explained,
and such a fortunate journey,
and having seen these wonders of the world,
it was best to end now, before bad luck could hunt him down.
Smiling at Caesar, gleaming with oil, perfumed with roses,
naked, he leapt into the pyre,
and never made a sound.

"The Athenians inscribed this on his tomb:
*Zarmanus, a traveller from India, has immortalised himself according to the
    custom of his country, here he lies.*"

– So writes Nicolaus of Damascus,
there is no reason to doubt him.

Strabo, Geography, *XV. 1. 72–73*

RULES OF THE GAME

Success requires close attention to questions asked by other players.

You may not ask for a card in your own hand.

At any time you may ask what was the last question, who asked it, what was the answer.

Any question prior to the last is History, and may not be discussed.

Paper and writing instruments may not be used to record the game.

Sometimes it is correct to ask questions to which you're already certain the answer is "no", so as to pass this knowledge to your allies.

A perfect history of the game thus far is worth more than perfect logic based on partial knowledge.

THE HOTEL

It's a strange time of night, I have just arrived at my hotel, I am waiting to check in. Porters hurry past, ignoring me and my small suitcase.

My friend surprises me.

"You here?"

"Of course," she says, "I've been looking for you. J is here too."

At once I'm annoyed. "Why is he here?"

"He says he has all of your letters, and he wants to give them back."

"What letters? I never wrote to him."

"Nonetheless, he wants to give them back. Also the photographs, and the manuscript of your disowned novel."

I have always been careful never to write a novel.

Now I'm not sure what infuriates me more: J's false claim that I wrote to him, or the fact that I'll have to take possession of these documents, carry them away in my small suitcase, file them among my papers at home, already too voluminous.

ARS POETICA

The birds in their passage are always observed to fly against the wind; hence the great contention among the bird-catchers which shall gain the wind; if it is westerly, the bird-catcher who lays his net most to the east is sure of the most plentiful sport. The birds are enticed to alight by captive call-birds: generally five or six linnets, two gold-finches, two green-finches, one wood-lark, one red-poll, and per-haps a bull-finch, a yellow-hammer, a tit-lark, and a siskin. These are placed at small distances from the nets in little cages. The bird-catcher has besides what he calls his flur-birds, which are tied upon a moveable perch, which the bird-catcher can raise at pleasure by means of a string; these he lifts gently up and down as the wild bird approaches. But this is not enough to allure the wild bird down; it must be called by one of the call-birds in the cages; and these, by being made to moult prematurely in a warm cage under blankets, call louder and more piercingly than those that are at freedom. There even appears a malicious joy in these call-birds to bring the wild ones into the same state of captivity. Their sight and hearing far exceed those of the bird-catcher; for, the instant the wild birds are per-ceived, the intelligence is given by one to the rest of the call-birds, who all unite in an ecstasy of pleasure. The call-birds do not sing a continuous note, but incite the wild ones by short jerks, which may be heard at a great distance. The allurement of this call has such a power, that the wild bird hearing is stopped in its most rapid flight; and lights boldly within twenty yards of the bird-catcher, on a spot it would otherwise never consider. This is the opportunity wished for, and the bird-catcher pulling a string, the nets on each side rise in an instant, and clap directly down on the little victim. It frequently happens that if half a flock only are caught, the remaining half will immediately afterwards light between the nets, and share the fate of their companions. Should only one bird escape, this unhappy survivor will also venture into danger till it is caught; such a fascinating power have the call-birds.

Goldsmith, A History of the Earth and Animated Nature

76

BECAUSE THE WORLD IS ROUND

What colour is a pound of neutrons? Why do nosebleeds stop? If you went to the bottom of the ocean and cut open a fibre-optic cable and looked into the end of it, would the light be bright enough to blind you? Do animals know or care if we are naked? Are roses somehow not the same as other flowers? How many potato chips would it take to stop a bullet? Is existential dread a natural phenomenon? Can snakes move their eggs? If you drink a shot of vodka after brushing your teeth, do you have to brush them again? Do famous people introduce themselves to each other? What kind of gosling is this? If you were falling in an endless pit could you fall asleep? What is the coldest star we know about? Is there such a thing as being too small to fit through an exit? What is a "leopard head town"? If a helicopter could hover for 24 hours straight, would the entire earth rotate beneath it? What happens if you watch a movie in your dream that you've never seen before? Why don't we sneeze in our sleep? If I held some soil and a seed in my bare hand for long enough, could I grow a tree?

MY PERSONAL INVOLVEMENT

there was a laser beam that
came through the window; hit
famous customers

. This sort of desire
is what makes me want to get up early in the morning.

People just threw up their hands and
asked, The nostalgia question

It's so com-
mon now, because every ten-year-old kid has
Walter Benjamin
"watching the same channel"

A SIMPLE PLAN

"Then the captain came out

: It was late, and they were looking
for something else—

cash in every closet. The obligatory

Five down.

Finnegans Wake.

scene of an escape

, because that's what friends are for.

the game is seriously

MORE OF THE SAME

We are living, in fact,

La Reprise

"un peu plus de bru- *talité."*

"Just a side order of love,"

And

you only have maybe five seconds of revelation."

ARS POETICA

Dear friends,

I forget which country I wrote you from before.
Thanks for the map, no one else here has one.

Please send me *Metalworking* by Monge, 10 francs.
Merly's *Carpentry* with 140 diagrams.
The Illustrated Book of Forestry Sawmills, 3 francs, 128 pictures.
Piloting Steamboats, *Powders and Saltpetres*,
The Little Woodworker, *Operating Mines*,
Guide to Gunmaking, *Glassmaker's Manual*,
Textiles, *Artesian Wells*.

Hydraulics for Beginners, *The Sky* by Guillemin,
The Department of Longitudes Annual, 1882.
Jacquet's *Planning Arches*, Debauve's *Underground Passages*, 1 volume.
Also *A Complete Treatise on Railways* by Couch,
chez Dunod, quai des Augustins,
and the *Manual for Manufacturing Precision Instruments*.

Soon I will turn thirty. Hope for the best.

Why haven't you sent me Bonniceau's *Building at Sea*
and Kaltbrünner's *Traveller's Manual* from Reinwald and Co.,
     15 rue des Saints-Pères?
I also require catalogues of pyrotechnics,
mechanical models, novelties, and magic.
A pocket theodolite (if it costs no more than 1,800 francs),
a mineralogical kit with 300 samples,
a half-pound of beetroot powder.
Also look in my Arabic papers for a folder called *Jokes and Games*.

Whatever happens, buy the books.
The days and even the nights are too long.

Above all, <u>buy the theodolite</u>.

Enclosed: self-portrait in a banana garden.
My hair is turning white every day.

Do you prefer I come home? Please say no.
I am yours alone,

A.

Rimbaud, Letters, *23 May, 1880–21 April, 1890*

ARS POETICA

For want of a stove I bought three quarts of vermouth di Torino.

Last summer I drank milk every night except three. But here I am too lonely.

The landlady says no guinea pigs: they pee too much.

Shall I buy an owl?

The first screech owl mocked me, and died after one hour. He pretended to be hungry, devoured a goldfinch, perfidiously waited till I turned my back,

then dropped dead.

At least I am still working, with my legs.

What is left for me now? Only the future.

Klee, Italian Diary, *October 1901–May 1902*

Circa 1855

Accumulators.
Advantages of travel.
Agates for striking sparks.
Agreement with servants.
Alarm gun.
Alloy for bullets.
Alkail.
Almanack (see Diagram).
Alpenstock.
Alphabet, signal.
Alpine tent.
Amadou.
Ammunition (see Gun-fittings and Ammunition).
Anastatic process.
Anchors.
Andersson, Mr.
Angareb (bedstead).
Angles, to measure; by means of chords.
Animal heat.
Anthills of white ants, as ovens; yellow ants, as signs of direction.
Arctic (see Snow, Esquimaux, and Climbing and Mountaineering).
Arms, weapons.
Arrows; set by a springe; to poison; to shoot fish.
Artificial horizon.
Ashes, for soap; for salt; for saltpetre and touchpaper; bivouac in; in flooring; dressing skins.
Ass; kicking, to check; braying.
Atkinson, Mr.
Austin, Mr.
Autographic ink.
Awnings, to boat; to litter; to tents.
Axe, for marking trees; for ice; to re-temper.
Axletree, to mend; to prepare wood for.
Backs, sore.
Bags for sleeping in; saddle-bags; bags carried over saddle; on packsaddle; to tie the mouth of.
Baines, Mr.
Baker, Sir S.
Baking Ball (bullet); poisoned (see Lead).
Ballantyne, Mr.
Bamboo rafts; to dig with; to cut meat; to strike sparks; to boil water in; to hitch together.
Barclay, Captain, of Ury.
Bark, to strip; for boats; for water vessels; for string and cord; for cloth.
Barrels, as water vessels; in digging wells; to make filters; as floats (see also Gourd-floats).
Barth, Dr.
Basket-work boats; bucket; to

Bows set by a spring (see Arrows).

Box of card, to pack flat.

Braces, for trousers; for saddlery; to weave.

Brands, for trees; for cattle.

Break to carriage wheels.

Breakwater of floating spars.

Bridges of felled trees; flying bridges.

Bridles.

Broken limbs.

Brush, to make; paint-brush.

Buccaneer.

Bucket; pole and bucket at wells.

Buckle.

Bullet; poisoned (see Lead).

Buoys.

Burning down trees; hollows in wood.

Burning-glasses.

Bush-costume.

Bush-laws.

Bushing a tent.

Butcher Butcher's knife.

Butter; relieves thirst.

Caches and Depots – caches; hiding jewels; depositing letters; reconnoitring by help of porters.

Caesar.

Calabash floats; water vessels.

Calculations, to procure; blank forms.

Calf stuffed with hay (Tulchan).

Campbell, Mr. J., of Islay.

Camel.

Camp (see Bivouac, Hut, Tent), to fortify; camp fire; baking beneath.

Candles and Lamps – candles; materials for candles; candlesticks; lamps to obtain a blaze in early morning.

Canoe, of a log; of three planks; of reeds and fibre; of bark; of the Rob Roy pattern; to carry on horseback.

Canvas, life-belt; water vessels; boat; painted, for sleeping rug.

Cap (hat); (percussion); to obtain fire from.

Carbon paper for tracing.

Carcass (carrion), to find; newly dead animal, warmth of.

Card-boxes, to pack flat.

Carpenters' tools (see Burning down Trees.

Carrara, shipping heavy blocks.

Carriages – wagons; drays; tarring wheels; breaks and drags; sledges; North American travel (trail); palanquins.

Carrion.

Carross (fur).

Cartel (bedstead).

Carter, Alpine Outfitter.

Case-hardening.

Cask (see Barrel).

Castings, of lead; cast-steel.

Cats cannot endure high altitudes.

Catgut; for nooses.

Cattle – weights carried by cattle; theory of loads and distances;

horses; mules; asses; oxen; cows; camels; dogs; goats and sheep; management of horses and other cattle; intelligence of, in finding water; smell road; keep guard; will efface cache marks; to water cattle; to swim with; to use as messengers (see Horse).

Cattle-dung, as fuel; as tinder; in plastering huts; in making floors; in dressing skins.

Catlin, Mr.

Caulking boats; leaky water vessels.

Caviare.

Cerate ointment.

Chaff, to cut, with a sickle.

Chairs.

Chalk to mark hats of beaters; whitewash.

Charcoal, to make; for gunpowder; in balls (gulo); fireplace for; used in filters; pencils made of; powdered and buried as a mark; animal charcoal.

Cheese, to make.

Chill, radiation (see Vital Heat, Wet Clothes, and Comfort in Travel).

Chisel, cold for metals or stone.

Chollet's dried vegetables.

Chords, table of; table for triangulation by.

Christison, Dr., tables on diet.

Chronometer (see Watch-pocket).

Clay for pottery.

Cleanliness (see Washing Clothes; Washing Oneself; Warmth of Dirt).

Cliffs, to descend with ropes.

Climbing and Mountaineering – climbing; descending cliffs with ropes; leaping poles and ropes; the art of climbing difficult places; snow mountains; ropes; ice-axe; alpenstock; boots, spectacles, and masks – climbing with a horse; descending with wagons; rarefied air, effect of; mountains, coup e'air on; magnetism of.

Clothing – materials; warmth of different kinds; waterproofing and making incombustible, sewing materials; articles of dress (caps, coats, socks, etc.); wet clothes, to dry; to keep dry; washing clothes; soap; washing flannels; washing oneself; warmth of dirt; bath glove and brush; double clothing for sleeping in.

Clove-hitch.

Coat; to carry.

Cold (see Chill).

Collar, horse; swimming-collar.

Colomb and Bolton's signals.

Comfort in travel; dry clothes.

Compass.

Conclusion of the Journey – completing collections;

alphabetical lists; observations re-calculated; lithographical map.

Concrete for floors.

Condiments.

Condors, to trap.

Convergence of tracks aflight, to water; to dead game; of bees to hive.

Cooking; utensils; fire-places; ovens; cook to be quick in making the fire.

Cooper, Mr. W. M.

Copper, to cover with tin; copper boats.

Cormorants.

Corracles.

Cord, String, Thread – substitutes; sewing; needles, to make (see Ropes).

Corks and stoppers.

Cot.

Cotton, for clothing; for tinder.

Counting, as done by savages.

Coverlets.

Cows.

Crawfurd, Mr. J.

Cresswell, Lieut., R.N.

Crocodiles, to shoot.

Cross, as a mark for roads.

Crowbar.

Crows, to destroy.

Crupper.

Culprits, to secure; punishment.

Cumming, Mr. Gordon.

Cups; to make tea in.

Curing meat; hides.

D's for saddle.

Dahoman night-watch.

Dalyell, Sir R.

Dana, Mr.

Dangers of travel.

Darwin, Mr.

Dateram (for tent and picket ropes).

Davenport brothers.

Death of one of the party.

Decoy-ducks.

Defence.

Depot (see Caches and Depots).

Dew, to collect for drinking.

Diagram of altitudes and bearings.

Dial, sun.

Diarrhoea.

Diet, theory of.

Digging.

Dirt, warmth of.

Discipline.

Diseases.

Distances, to measure; travelled over by day; loads and distances, theory of.

Distilling.

Division of game; by drawing lots.

Doebereiner and Oelsner.

Dogs, in harness; in fishing; in finding water; as messengers; to keep at bay; eating snow; sheep-dogs.

Donkey (see Ass).

Douglas, Sir H.

Down of plants as tinder.

recover a lost line; otters; boat-fishing; to see things under water; nets; spearing fish; intoxicating fish; otters, cormorants, and dogs; fish roe as food; fish, dried and pounded; fish skin (see Skin); fish-hook for springes.

Fitzroy, Admiral.

Flags, for signals.

Flannel; to wash.

Flash of sun from mirror.

Flashing signals.

Flashing alphabet.

Flask, battered, to mend.

Fleas.

Flies, near cattle-kraals.

Flints; for gun; sparks used as a signal; as a light to show the road; flint knives.

Floats; floating powers of wood.

Flogging.

Floors, to make.

Flour, nutritive value; to carry.

Flying bridges.

Food – nutritive elements of food; food suitable for stores; condiments; butcher; store-keeping; wholesome food procurable in bush; revolting food, to save lives of starving men; cooking utensils; fire-places for cooking; ovens; bush-cookery.

Forbes, Captain, R.N.

Forbes, Professor J.

Fords and Bridges – fords; swamps; passing things from hand to hand; plank roads; snow-drifts and weak ice; bridges; flying bridges.

Forge.

Forest as shelter; log huts; to travel in a straight line through forests.

Form, for log-book; calculations; for agreement with servants.

Fortification of camp.

Fountains.

Fuel; heating powers of various kinds.

Fulminating powder in destroying wolves; percussion caps.

Furniture – bed; hammocks and cots; mosquito-nets; chairs; table.

Fuses, in making a fire.

Gall (ox-gall); girth-galls; blisters.

Game, other means of capturing (besides shooting) – general remarks; springes; pitfalls; traps; poison; bird-line; catching with the hand; bolas; lasso; ham-stringing; hawking; to hide from animals of prey; division of spoils; to float across a river; to carry dead animals, to find; water, in paunch of.

Garibaldi.

Gauze, for mosquito-curtains; to make incombustible; stretched over mercurial horizon.

Geographical Society.

Gilby, Mr.

Gipsy tent; marks (patterans).

Girths; girth-galls.

Glass, to shape; substitute for, in mercurial horizon; to silver; substitute for glass.

Glaisher, Mr.

Glaze for pottery.

Glove (bath-glove).

Glue.

Goats.

Gold, to carry.

Gourd float; boat (makara).

Grains (for spearing fish).

Grant, Captain.

Grass shutters.

Graters.

Grease for leather; in dressing skins; for wheels; to procure from bones; for relieving thirst; oiling the person; butter; olive oil, to purify.

Gregory, Mr.

Gul (ball of charcoal).

Gum.

Gun-fittings and Ammunition – Powder-flask; percussion-caps; wadding; flints; gunpowder; bullets; shot and slug.

Guns and Rifles – breech-loading; best size of gun; sights, ramrod, etc.; rust; olive-oil, to purify; injuries to gun, to repair; guns to hang up; to carry on a journey; on horse-back; to dispose of at night; to clean; to procure fire; to set an alarm-gun; to support tenting.

Gunpowder, to make; to carry; mark on stone left by flash; in lighting a fire; in making touch-paper; substitute for salt; fulminating powder to kill beasts; powder-flask; battered, to mend.

Gut; catgut.

Gutta percha (see Macintosh).

Guy-rope in tenting.

Haemorrhage.

Haggis.

Hall, Dr. Marshall.

Hammering, sound of.

Hammock.

Hamstringing.

Handing things across a swamp.

Handbook for Field Service.

Handkerchief, to sling a jar; to tie the wrists.

Hands of prisoner, to secure.

Harness – saddles for riding; bags; sore backs; pack-saddles; pack-bags; art of packing; girths, stirrups, bridles, etc.; tethers, hobbles and knee-halters; horse-collar, traces and trek-tows.

Hats Hawker, Colonel.

Hawks for hawking; to trap.

Head, Sir F.

Hearne, Mr.

Heat, vital; heating power of different fuels (see Fire).

Heather in bivouac.

Heavy bodies, to move.

Heber, Bishop.

Heliostat.

Helm.

Hides (see Skins; also Leather).

Hiding-places (see Caches and Depots).

Hills (see Climbing, etc.).

Hitch, Malay (see Knots).

Hobbies.

Holes, to dig.

Honey, to find; honey-bird.

Hooker, Dr.

Hooks, for walls of hut; fish-hooks; for springes.

Horizon, artificial.

Horn; substitute for glass; powder-horn.

Horse; to check descent of wagon; tied to sleeping master; to horn of dead game; picketted to a dateram; running by side of; climbing with; descending with; in deep snow; swimming with; carrying a gun on; loading on; tying a prisoner on; raising water from wells; horseflesh; hair for string; collar.

Hostilities – to fortify a camp; weapons to resist an attack; natives forbidden to throng the camp; keeping watch; prairie set on fire; tricks upon robbers; passing through a hostile country; securing prisoners; proceedings in case of death.

Hours' journey.

Huber, M.

Hue and Gabet, MM.

Hunger.

Huts – log huts; underground huts; snow-houses; wattle and daub; palisades; straw or reed walls; bark; mats; Malay hitch; tarpaulin; whitewash; roofs, floors, windows.

Ice, weak, to cross; axe; burning lens, made of.

Incombustible stuffs.

Index, to make.

India-rubber (see MacIntosh).

Information, preparatory, to obtain; through native women.

Ink; autographic; sympathetic.

Insects as food; mosquitos; flies; fleas; lice.

Instruments for surveying; verification of; porters for; surgical instruments.

Interpreters.

Intestine to carry water; as swimming-belt; to make catgut from; membrane thread.

Iron, ore to reduce; forge; boats.

Isinglass.

Ivory, to sling on pack-saddle.

Jar, to sling.

Jackson, Colonel.

Javelins, set over beast paths.

Jerked meat.

Jewels, to secrete.

Jourt, Kirghis.

Kabobs.

Kane, Dr.
Kegs for pack-saddles.
Keels.
Kerkari.
Kettle; used for distilling.
Kite, as a signal.
Knapsack sleeping-bag; to carry heavy weights knapsack fashion.
Knee-halter.
Knife.
Knots – see also Knots in Alpine Ropes; tying to tent-pole; tent-pole, to mend; knotting neck of a bag; Malay hitch; matting and weaving; raft fastening; leather vessels, to mend; hide lashings; rush chairs. For a place to make fast to, see Burning down Trees; Digging Holes to plant them; Dateram.
Kraals.
Ladder.
Laird, M'Gregor, Mr.
Lamp; of lead, to cast; Esquimaux; lamp-black.
Lantern.
Lappar (to scare game).
Lashings of raw hide.
Lasso.
Lathe.
Laws of the bush.
Lead; to cast.
Leaks, to caulk, in boats; in water vessels.
Leaping-ropes and poles.
Leather – to dress hides; to preserve them without dressing; greasing leather; leather clothing; tents; lashings of raw hide; leather vessels, to repair; ropes (see Skins).
Leggings.
Leichhardt, Dr.
Length, measurement of.
Letters, to deposit; carried by animals; of alphabet, to stamp and to brand.
Lever.
Lice.
Lime, to make; to poison fish; bird-lime.
Linen clothing.
Lines, for fishing.
Lists of stores; of instruments; alphabetical, to make.
Lithographic map, to make.
Litter for the wounded; horse-litter.
Livingstone, Dr.
Lloyd, Mr.
Loading guns.
Loads and distances, theory of.
Locusts, to cook.
Log-book; log for a boat's speed; log-hut.
Lopstick (to mark a road).
Lost road; articles in sand; fishing-line, in water; to see things lost under water.
Lots, how to draw.
Lucan, Lord.
Lucifer matches; for percussion caps.

Lunars.

Luxuries of tent-life.

Lye (for soap).

Lunch, Lieutenant.

McClintock, Captain Sir L.

Macgregor, Mr.

Macintosh for under bedding; sleeping-bag; inflatable boats; water vessels; gun-cover; is spoilt by grease.

Maclear, Sir Thos.

McWilliams, Dr.

Madrina (of mules).

Magnetic bearings; magnetism of rocks.

Makara (gourd-raft).

Malaria fever.

Malay hitch.

Marks for the way-side – marks in the forest; for canoe routes; marks with stones; gipsy and other marks; paint to mark cattle (see also Caches).

Mask for snow mountains.

Mast, substitute for.

Match, lucifer; sulphur.

Mats; for tents (see Reed huts).

Mattresses; feathers for.

Meaden, Captain J.

Measurements – distance travelled; of rate of movement; tables for ditto; natural units; measurement of angles; chords and table of; triangulation; table for, on principle of chords; time, measurement of.

Meat biscuit.

Mechanical appliances – on land; by wetted seeds; accumulation of efforts; to raise weights out of water.

Medicine – general remarks; drugs and instruments; bush remedies; illnesses and accidents; litter for the wounded (see also Palanquin).

Membrane, Sinew, Horn – parchment; cat-gut; membrane thread; sinews for thread; glue; isinglass; horn, tortoise-shell and whalebone.

Memoranda and Log-books – general remarks; pocket MS.-book; log-book; calculation books; number of observations requiring record; memoranda, to arrange.

Metals – fuel for forge; bellows; iron and steel; case-hardening; lead, to cast; tin-plates; copper.

Mercury to harden lead with.

Metallic (prepared) paper.

Miller, Professor W. H.

Milk, to preserve; sizing paper with; used as sympathetic ink; to milk wild cows.

Milton, Lord.

Mirage.

Mirror, signalling with the sun.

Mitchell, Sir Thomas.

Moltke.

Mosquito curtains; tent of.

Moss on trees, a sign of direction.

Mould for candles.

Mountain (see Climbing and Mountaineering).

Muddy water, to filter.

Muff.

Mule.

Murray, Admiral Hon. C.

Nails, substitutes for.

Napoleon I, on bivouac.

Natives (see Savages).

Navy (British) diet.

Needles.

Neighing.

Nets.

Nettle as food.

Niger, expedition to.

Night, to follow a track by; shooting; night-glass; compass.

Nocturnal animals.

Nooses.

Notes, to keep.

Notices to another party.

Number of a party; to camps.

Nunn, W. and Co.

Nutritive elements of food.

Oakum, for bedding.

Observations, number required; to procure calculation of.

Occultations, telescopes for.

Oil (olive) to refine (see Grease).

Ointment.

Opera glass as a night glass; supplies a burning lens; as a lens to condense light.

Ophthalmia.

Organising an Expedition – best size for party; servants' engagement; women.

Osborn, Captain Sherard, R.N.

Ostrich eggs, to carry.

Oswell, Mr. W. C.

Otter; fishermen's board.

Outfit – stores for general use; for individual use; presents and articles for payment; summary; means of transport; outfit of medicine; Alpine gear; sewing materials.

Outline forms for calculations; for the log-book.

Outrigger, to balance canoes; irons for oars.

Ovampo camp-fires.

Ovens.

Owen, Professor.

Ox; for stalking; ox-gall.

Paces, length of; to measure rate of travel by.

Pack saddles; kegs for; art of packing.

Padlock to a buckled strap.

Palliasse.

Paint; to paint cattle; paint-brush.

Palanquin (see Litter).

Palisades.

Palliser, Captain J.

Pan-hunting.

Paper; warmth of, in coverlet.

Parbuckling.

Parchment.

Park, Mungo.

Parkyns, Mansfield, Mr.

Party, to organise (see Organising

an Expedition).

Paste.

Patch to a water-bag.

Path, lost.

Patterans (gipsy marks by road).

Paunch of dead animal, water in.

Payment, articles of.

Peal, Mr.

Peat.

Pegs, tent; to secure tent ropes; for hooks.

Pemmican.

Pencils.

Pendulum.

Pens.

Percussion caps.

Pereira, Dr.

Picketting horses in sand.

Picture writing.

Pillow.

Pitch.

Pitching a tent.

Pitfall.

Pith for tinder; for hats.

Plaids in bivouac in heather; wetted, in wind.

Planks, to sew together (see Timber); plank-roads.

Poaching devices (see Game, Other Means, etc.).

Poison for beasts; for fish; for stakes in pitfalls; for arrows; for bullets; snake bites; suspicion of poison; poisonous plants; antidotes to poison.

Pole for tent; pole and bucket; pole star.

Poncho.

Portable food.

Porters for instruments; of provisions for depots.

Pottery – glaze for; clay; pots for stores and caches; pot for cooking; to mend; substitute for; baking in; distilling from.

Powder (see Gunpowder).

Prairie on fire.

Precautions against poison; malaria; unwholesome water; thieves.

Preparatory Inquiries – qualifications for a traveller; dangers of travel; advantages; to obtain information; conditions of failure and success; the leader; servants.

Presents for savages.

Preserving food.

Pricker for gun-nipples.

Prisoners, to secure; punishment.

Pulley.

Pump.

Puna (effect of high mountain air).

Punishment.

Punt of hide; of tin.

Putrid water.

Pyrites.

Qualifications for a traveller.

Quicksilver, to harden lead.

Quills, to prepare; to carry letters; to hold minute specimens.

Quinine.

Radiation chill.

Rae, Dr.

Rafts and boats – rafts of wood; of bamboo; boating power of woods; burning down trees; rafts of reeds; of hide; of gourds (Makara); rude boats; sailing; log canoe; of three planks; inflatable india-rubber; of basket; of reed of fibre; of hide; corracle and fibre; of hide; corracle and skin punt; bark boat and canoe; tin boat; boats, well built, of various materials; boating gear; boat building; boat management; awning (see also Boats).

Rain, to catch.

Ramrod; to replace; probing with, for water; broken ramrod tubes.

Rank birds, to prepare for eating.

Rarefied air.

Rarey, Mr.

Rate of movement, to measure; of swimming; theory of load, and rate of travel.

Rations; of water.

Raw meat; as an antiscorbutic.

Reconnoitring arid lands.

Reeds, for rafts; mats; huts and fences; to weave; for pens; as a cache (see Bamboo).

Reel, substitute for.

Reflectors, to light tinder; of sun for a signal.

Remedies.

Resin.

Retreat, hurried.

Richardson, Sir J.; Mr.

Rifle (see Guns and Rifles).

Right angle, to lay out.

Rings for saddle.

Rivers, to cross (see Fords and Bridges); their banks are bad roads.

Road, to mark; plank-road; lost road.

Rob Roy canoe.

Robbers (see Thieves).

Robbiboo.

Rock, a reservoir of heat at night; magnetism of.

Rockets.

Roe of fish, as food.

Roofs.

Ropes, for descending cliffs; Alpine; of sheeting; of bark (see Cord, String, Thread); tying a prisoner.

Rudder.

Rumford, Count.

Running, with horses.

Rushes (see Reeds), for chairs.

Rust.

Sack (see Rag).

Saddle; packsaddle; saddle as pillow; saddle bags; as screens against wind.

Sails to raft; sail-tent.

Salt; given to cattle; salt-lick; salt meat; to make; to salt hides; to prepare salt meat for cooking (see Sea-water).

Saltpetre; for gunpowder.

Sand, sleeping in; to pitch tents or picket horses in; ripple marks on, give sign of direction; used in raising a sarcophagus.

Sarcophagus, raised by sand.

Savages, management of – general remarks; bush laws; to enable a savage to keep count; drawing lots.

Saw mark.

Scarecrow.

Scent of human touch.

Schlagintweit, H.

Science, preparatory information in.

Scorpion sting.

Scurvy.

Sea-birds, as food – sea-water, wetting with, a remedy for thirst; a remedy for damp through rain; to distill.

Seaweed as fuel; as food; as fodder; as string; to make gum; its ashes.

Seeds wetted, expansive force of.

Sealing-wax varnish.

Seamanship.

Seasoning wood.

Sedlitz powders.

Servants.

Sewing.

Sextant, to learn the use of; glasses to re-silver.

Shavings for bedding.

Sheep; sheep dogs.

Sheets used as ropes.

Shelter from wind; from sky.

Shingle, bivouac on.

Shingles (wood tiles).

Shirt sleeves, how to tuck up; writing notes upon.

Shoes; of untanned leather, eatable; shoemakers' wax.

Shooting, hints on – how to load; shooting in water; night shooting; battues to mark the beaters; scarecrows; stalking horses; pan-hunting; the rush of an enraged animal; hiding game; tying up the shooting horse; division of game; duck shooting; crocodile shooting; tracks; carrying game; setting a gun as a spring-gun; bow and arrows; knives; night-glass.

Shot; for defence.

Shutters of grass.

Sickness (see Medicine).

Sickle, in cutting chaff.

Sights of a gun; to replace.

Signals – flashing with flags; reflecting the sun with a mirror; fire and smoke; other signals; letters carried by animals.

Signets.

Sinew-thread.

Size, for paper.

Skins (see Leather), eatable when untanned; salting animals in their own skins; baking them, ditto; boiling, ditto; skin rafts;

boats; water bags; lashings of raw hide; to make glue.

Sky, shelter from.

Sledge.

Sleeping-bags – knapsack bags; Arctic bags; peasants' sack.

Slippers.

Slugs (shot); to cast.

Smell of road; of water; of human touch; of a Negro; as an indication to stop.

Smith, Archibald, Mr.

Smith, Dr.

Smith's work.

Smoke signals; smoking skins.

Snake bites; tree snakes in boating; poison for arrows.

Snards.

Snow, bivouac on; huts of; hearth on; filter for muddy water; snow does not satisfy thirst; blindness and spectacles; drifts to cross; ripple marks to steer by; snowy mountains, to climb.

Soap.

Socks.

Solder for tin.

Soldering (lots).

Sore backs to horses.

Sound, velocity of; signals by.

Span, measure of length; of angles.

Sparks; to strike; to make a fire from; struck as a signal; to show the road by night.

Spears, for fish; set over beast paths; trailed through grass by savages; to straighten wood for.

Specific gravities of wood.

Spectacles for snow; for seeing under water.

Speke, Captain.

Spokeshave.

Sponge, lapping up water from puddles; dew from leaves.

Spontaneous combustion.

Spoons.

Spring gun; bow.

Springes.

Squaring (right angles to lay out).

Stalking-horses and screens; stalking game.

Stars for bearings.

Starving men.

Steels for flints; steel tools; cast steel; case-hardening.

Sticks, small, for lighting fires; for fire by rubbing; for tenting purposes and substitutes; to bend or straighten.

Still (distilling).

Sting of scorpions and wasps.

Stirrups.

Stitches.

Stockings.

Stones, heated, to make water boil; as weapons of defence; as marks by roadside; to chisel marks upon.

Stool.

Stoppers.

Stores, lists of; store-keeping.

Tin; tin boat.
Tinder; tinder-boxes.
Toggle and strop.
Toilet in travel.
Tools.
Toothache.
Tortoiseshell.
Touchwood; touch-paper.
Tourniquet.
Tow rope, to fix.
Traces (harness).
Tracing designs.
Tracks, convergence of, towards water; towards dead game; to prepare ground to receive tracks; to obliterate tracks.
Transport, means of.
Trapping.
Travail (North America).
Travel, rate of.
Trees (see Timber), as shelter; to mark; to fell with fire; to hollow with fire; as signs of neighbouring water; to climb; to steer by; to make caches in; boughs bent as accumulators; bark to strip; tree-bridges.
Trektows (traces).
Triangulation; table for, by chords.
Trenches, for cooking.
Trimmers.
Trous de loup.
Trousers.
Tschudi, Dr.
Tulchan bishops.
Turf screen against wind.

Turnscrew in pocket-knife.
Turpentine.
Turtle, water in its pericardium.
Tylor, Mr.
Tyndall, Professor.
Uganda thorn-wreath.
Ulysses.
Underground huts.
Units of length.
Ure's *Dictionary*.
Vapour baths.
Varnish of sealing-wax.
Vavasour, Lady.
Vegetables, Chollet's.
Vegetation indicates water.
Verification of instruments.
Vermin on the person.
Vessels to carry water, small; large.
Vice in horses; in oxen.
Virgil.
Vital heat.
Vraic (see Seaweed).
Vulture trapping.
Wadding.
Wafers.
Wagons; to take across a river; axle-tree, to repair.
Waistcoat; strait-waistcoat.
Wakefulness.
Walls; of snow; of straw or reeds.
Washing clothes; oneself.
Watch, pocket for; watch-glass as a burning lens; cover as a reflector.
Watching.
Water for Drinking – general remarks; signs of the

neighbourhood of water; pools of water; fountains; wells; snow-water; distilled water; occasional means of quenching thirst; to purify water that is muddy or putrid; thirst, to relieve; small water-vessels; kegs and tanks; to raise water from wells for cattle; to see things under water; shooting by waterside; floating game across water; raising heavy bodies out of water; banks of watercourse a bad pathway; bivouac by water; water causes earth over caches to sink; waterproofing.

Wattle and daub.

Wax, bee-hives, to find; waxed paper; wax candles; shoemakers' wax.

Way, to find – recollection of a path; to walk in a straight line through forest; to find the best way down a hill-side; blind paths; lost in a fog; mirage; lost path; theory.

Weapons of defence.

Weaving mats; girths.

Webbing.

Weber, Dr.

Weights drawn and carried by cattle; theory of, and distances; heavy weights, to move; to carry.

Welding iron.

Wells; dry, used as sleeping places.

Wet clothes, to dry (see Dry).

Whalebone.

Wheels, to tar and grease; tire made of hide.

Whistle.

Whitewash.

Whymper, Mr.

Williams, Rev. Mr.

Wind, shelter from; as a guide.

Women, strength of; kindliness of.

Wood (see Timber and Trees) shavings for bed; fire-wood; wooden cups for tea; shingles for roof.

Woolley, Mr.

Wounded persons, to carry.

Wrangel, Admiral.

Writing Materials – paper; bookbinding; pens and paintbrushes; ink; ox-gall; wafers, paste, and gum; signets; sealing-wax varnish; small boxes for specimens; letters, to deposit en cache; writing in the dark; on horseback.

Wyndham, Mr. F. M.

Zemsemiyah.

KING Q

A New World

They say after the last sun burned out
King Q was left in Mictlan, the graveyard of the world
(there was nowhere else to go),
where the bones of all the extincted peoples of all the former suns
make hills and valleys, so numberless are the dead.
It is time for a new world, thought King Q,
and I know how to breed it.
These bones need four kinds of blood.

Let us agree the science is uncertain,
but there are songs about this:
King Q, with his penknife, nicked his both earlobes,
his tongue, the tip of his (carefully) penis, his both calves,
and these were enough drops of blood to awaken the bones,
and these were bones enough to people the whole world,
the fifth world, as we count them, under the fifth sun,
blame it on King Q.

His Favourite House

So King Q's favourite house was his Toltec house,
there were four rooms.
The east room was wallpapered with gold.
That was the room for hard decisions.
The west room was wallpapered with real turquoise,
though King Q called it his chamber of jade.
That was the room for second thoughts.
The walls of the south room were covered with seashells:
the room for restless stirrings.
The north room was covered with red seashells:
that was the room where King Q tried to think consoling thoughts.

Oh, King Q had another favourite house: he called it his house of feathers. There were feathers sewn to all the walls, feathers sewn to the ceiling, the carpets were feathers underfoot. Yellow feathers, quetzal feathers, cotinga, white eagle, red spoonbill, red macaw. This was the house for reflecting that nothing lasts.

The Toltecs built the best houses, we all agree, but the Toltecs died and disappeared. Their perfect pots and perfect spoons and perfectly woven shirts are lost in the ground.

Between his houses was King Q's swimming pool, called Waters of Green Stones, also Fizzy Waters, and King Q made sure he was the only one who knew how to swim.

A Song of King Q

Rain so heavy, it knocks the birds from the sky.
Thunder sleeps deep inside the earth.
Sky so heavy, I knock my head / when I rise from my bed.

I sleep with a stone in my mouth
until one day I sleep with a tongue of stone
and a pillow stone almost the shape of my heart.

King of the Bands

Begin:

A pot of roucou rouge for lips.
Turmeric powder for eyelids.
Butterfly dust for brows.
Two serpent's fangs of jade.
A pearl under each tongue, and a lozenge of gold,
and a whistle of honey.
A beard of cotinga feathers, green as his birdsight,
and a bib of flamingo, scarlet as his nipples.
Turquoise goggles, carved from a single branch of stone,
and turquoise for his ears, little bells, his clavicles, his wrists and fingers.
A conch rattling with bees, that's for his loins,
and a belt of hide from the youngest rabbits,
buckle of mute cowrie.

Now bring his living wings, a pair for every pair of limbs,
iridescent and bristling like beetles.
Now hummingbird sandals, never to touch the ground.
At last his cape of rose hibiscus sewn,
a thousand petals shriveling by the half-minute,
delicate as the hue of bruise.

Summon mirrors.

Summon needles and birds.

Summon yellow bees and red bees and black bees.

Summon the twin who casts no shadow,
the twin of black glass,
his every inch of skin sticky as glass,
resin of pine and scorpion ash and centipede ash,
black as a mirror,

hungry sooty nectar:
twin of divine condiment.

Summon lightning from all five directions.

It is time to be famous.

There is almost no time left to be a king.

When It Was Over

After the pulque episode, King Q said it was over
– it is hard to be human, to balance the ways of eating and drinking,
    waking and sleeping, blaming and forgiving –
he locked up his books and instruments: there was nowhere to go
    but the sea.

He put on his feather drag and his beak of turquoise
and whispered a little fire on the shore
– driftwood burns in green and purple sizzles –
he counted his regrets and backward his blessings,
and as the sun rose and the blaze took heart, King Q sat down in the fire.

The smoke ascended green and purple and scarlet and orange and blue
– a dream of spoonbills and parrots,
macaws, contingas, herons –
and then it rained, and afterwards, in the ashes,
was a turquoise pebble almost the size of a fist.

So this is the legend of King Q.
They say he spent eight days in the Other Place,
busy with quartzes and hammers and broken glass,
then after eight mornings passed, there was a new star in the sky,
winking like a blue electric dart.
On the first of Alligator, he winks on old people;
on the first of Jaguar, he winks on small children,
ditto the first of Flower, the first of Deer;
on the first of Reed, he winks on dukes and princes;
on the first of Movement, he winks on the rest of the young;
on the first of Rain, he winks on the rain, and the rain dries up;
on the first of Water, he makes a drought;
on the first of Death, he winks on everyone, so bad luck all round.

As for King Q, he was born and died on his birthday,
then someone else came and lived in his house

and chewed his food and swallowed his milk and handed round
    his blessings, in a turquoise box or bowl
– the cousins, the wives, the sages, the magicians –
imagine you gave it all up for the life of an astronaut,
to dream the world like a fleet of birds,
only to find how wearisome is life in the sky,
wearisome, the life of a star, nothing to do but shine like a bad omen.

FLOWER SEASON

Before my tongue can name a flower,
my tongue is now a flower.
Before a hummingbird can stab
the soft mouth of a flower,
the knife in your hand is now a hummingbird.
Before I can fill my mouth with honey,
my tongue is a new meat flower.
The needle of every hummingbird
rejoices from my mouth,
my whole heart throbs with honey,
in this flower house I am drowning in honey,
my heart is alive with bees, drunk and formal.

Open all your throats! Boast all your honey,
divulging every pollen-tongue and velvet.
Crowned with bees, the hummingbird
is the tip of every new knife, thirsty for honey.
My honey life is a life of birds,
my honey throat is an ecstasy of bees all drowning.
Give them your tongue! Your scarlet flower
of meat, all this flower-living day.
Before my flower tongue is even ripe,
like a rain of tiny knives, the tiny gods of the air
descend in honey-fever, darts of honey.
Before my new mouth can even call this flower.

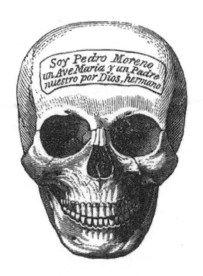

Soy Pedro Moreno
un Ave Maria y un Padre
nuestro por Dios, hermano

Usted también, pagano.

BECAUSE IT TURNS ME ON

How can I pet a crow?   Do islands ever drift?   What is the thing that knocks on my window at night?   Can we get vitamins from the moon?   Does my dog pretend to wag his tail to make me happy? Can you cut a colour in half?   Have I ever drunk the same molecule of water twice?   Does a gas mask work both ways?   Is it normal to forget my own face?   Why are people afraid of spiders when wasps are even more dangerous, and they can fly?   Is Elvis a bad name? Are there laws against starting an avalanche?   Do birds also get songs stuck in their heads?   If I were actually handsome and nobody told me, would I still know?   Is throwing money in the street considered littering?   How do you forget a taste?   Is any mammal green?   Is falling down the stairs as dangerous as they say?   Why does my brain do everything it does to keep me alive?

CLOSE COUNSEL

one's own authorship is
La Chambre

OSCURA ES EL AGUA

The first time I dreamt of drowning
I woke in a stranger's room
draped with black silk like a tomb
in a high and distant country,

its roof a single window
to a sky scarred with salt,
no one to name those stars.
Now I need never dream again of the sea.

Silvina Ocampo, Epitafio de un náufrago

A CONFESSION

I guess I'd rather be burnt alone
but drown with someone else,
if there's a choice.

IT'S GOOD THERE IS NO TSAR

I'm glad that Russia has no king,
glad that Russia is a fib,
glad that God is bored.

The sky is more real than the earth,
the stars are more real than the sky,
the years are bored as God.

I'm glad there are no people here,
all the mirror shows is black,
every book is blank.

These words could not mean any less.
There is no Russia left to help.
There is no God to thank.

Georgy Ivanov, Хорошо, что нет Царя

PETIT CARÊME

The natives have a name for this sharp wind.
It is tricky to pronounce, like the names of the dozen other winds.

Never before did I care about names for weather,
but one must have a hobby in this place.

Strange, they name the winds but not the rivers,
not the bridges, not the roads,
so no one can given directions without speaking a riddle.

*

Everyone here lives in the kind of house an owl would build
if an owl wanted to live in a house.

They use the same word for "house" and "bones left in the fire",
or different words but pronounced the same. Does it matter?

And the word for "flaw" is the same as "star",
so at night they say the sky is breaking,
and one day won't it be true?

COUSIN LAZARUS

*I eat the most famous vitamins
in the vitamin game.*

in two parts about the
(*Ambivalence,*

I'd give it to you if I could

"four times this week"

-shifting the stakes

"That's what makes it fun."

(*I'd give it to you,*

BIRTHDAY,

honeycomb

"pink noise"

SAY PLEASE

] burn rations [
] more is more [

Sappho, fragment 38

TONGUE LESSON

] bees never taste like honey [

Sappho, fragment 146

WHICH COMES FIRST

] black milk [
] or my eyes [

] sink or sleep [

Sappho, fragment 151

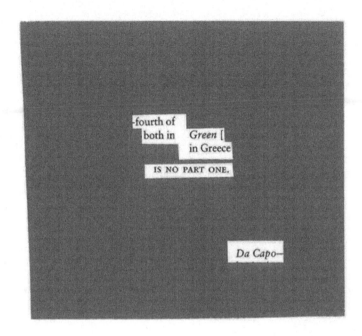

-fourth of
both in   *Green* [
             in Greece

IS NO PART ONE.

Da Capo—

131

AFTERWORD

My blood, I have discovered, is attractive and tasty to the ants, and they will come far out of their way to have it. These mornings I draw a little therefore, an eighth of an ounce or so, and using a sort of tiny aspergillum I sprinkle it on the floor near my desk. On cue, the ants stream in from the other rooms in meandering progression. As they swarm about the scattered drops, their gleeful thirst assumes a series of intricate patterns in continuous motion. These I closely observe, sketching rapidly with pencil and paper.

When, having consumed the blood away, the ants evacuate the room, I translate my sketches into passages of appropriate symbols, using specially prepared grids. Several stages of decoding, according to formulae I have with great effort and ingenuity devised, reveal my poems.

Of course the ants make me nervous: they know me too well after all, whereas I know next to nothing about them. I do not even know exactly where they come from, where they assemble, to which nest they carry their daily spoils of my flesh, if or how their minute appetites may ever be sated.

SOURCES

"Call it a little game between 'I' and 'me'" – Duchamp

The reader must have noticed that several of the texts in this book are found, appropriated, "readymade", or elsewise derived from existing sources; others are unfaithful translations, and my Ancient Greek and Nahuatl are imperfect. Here is a possibly incomplete list of books etc. from which *Enemy Luck* was made, in order of first reference:

Poems of Michael Drayton, ed. John Buxton (1953)

The Geography of Strabo, trans. H.C. Hamilton and W. Falconer (1903)

Incidents of Travel in Yucatan, John L. Stephens (1841)

The Tukuna, Curt Nimuendajú, trans. William D. Hohenthal (1952)

A History of the Earth, and Animated Nature, Oliver Goldsmith (1774)

The C.I.C. Annual 1920, St. Mary's College, Port of Spain

I Promise to Be Good: The Letters of Arthur Rimbaud, ed. and trans. Wyatt Mason (2003)

The Diaries of Paul Klee, 1898–1918, ed. Felix Klee, trans. Pierre B. Schneider, R.Y. Zachary, and Max Knight (1964)

The Art of Travel, Francis Galton (1872)

Anales de Cuauhtitlan, from the *Codex Chimalpopoca*, and *Historia general de las cosas de nueva España*, Bernardino de Sahagún, both trans. David K. Jordan (2006)

Cantares Mexicanos, trans. John Bierhorst (1985)

Silvina Ocampo, trans. Jason Weiss (2015)

"It's good that Russia has no Tsar", trans. Stephen Capus, in *The Penguin Book of Russian Poetry*, ed. Robert Chandler, Boris Dralyuk, and Irina Mashinski (2015)

If Not, Winter: Fragments of Sappho, trans. Anne Carson (2002)

"If there are other obligations that should be mentioned, let the present acknowledgement stand for them" – Berryman

THANKS

Actual writing – the business of pen, ink, notebook, and sometimes scissors – is a solitary and private matter. Before and after, one's imagination and vocabulary are provoked and nourished by conversation, reading, observation, travel – in these, other people are implicated. Both enemies and friends can be helpful, often in different ways. Luckily, my enemies are still outnumbered by my friends.

For their encouragement and criticism, for meals, drinks, and beds to sleep in, for companionship during travels and books to read and innumerable kinds of generosity, I'm grateful to Mary Adam, Lisa Allen-Agostini, Andre Bagoo, Alastair Bird, Vahni and Leila Capildeo, Kriston Chen, Loretta Collins Klobah, Christopher Cozier, Ifeona Fulani, David Iaconangelo, Kelly Baker Josephs, Fawzia Kane, Anu Lakhan, Sean Leonard, Shara McCallum, Annie Paul, Georgia Popplewell, Shivanee Ramlochan, Ashraph Ramsaran, Gemma Robinson and Rowan Cruft, Roxanne Ryce-Paul and Nicolas Touron, Marina Salandy-Brown (and all my colleagues at the Bocas Lit Fest, past and present), David Sasaki, Adalber Salas Hernández, Mark Searl, Damien Smith, Jeremy Taylor (and all my colleagues at *Caribbean Beat*), Anne Walmsley and Ron Farquhar, Joanna Woolman, and Georg Zipp.

It's impossible to imagine contemporary Caribbean literature without Jeremy Poynting, Hannah Bannister, and Peepal Tree Press. No thanks are adequate.

Writing, or for that matter anything else, would not be possible without my parents, Dian and Martin; without Simon and Natasha, Amelia and Aidan, Gisel, and Andrew.

ABOUT THE AUTHOR

Nicholas Laughlin is a writer and editor. He was born in Trinidad and has always lived there.

He is the editor of *The Caribbean Review of Books* and the arts and travel magazine *Caribbean Beat*; programme director of the Bocas Lit Fest, Trinidad and Tobago's annual literary festival; and co-director of the contemporary art space and network Alice Yard.

His first collection of poetry, *The Strange Years of My Life*, was published by Peepal Tree Press in 2015.

He has edited a volume of early essays by C.L.R. James, *Letters from London* (2003), and a revised, expanded edition of V.S. Naipaul's early family correspondence, *Letters Between a Father and Son* (2009).

ALSO BY NICHOLAS LAUGHLIN

The Strange Years of My Life
ISBN: 9781845232924; pp. 86; pub. 2015; £8.99

The troupe of "friends" and "strangers" whom the reader meets in these poems are sometimes alter egos, sometimes aliases, sometimes adversaries. Located in worlds such as those of French film noir, spy movies, and travellers' tales, they inhabit a milieu of mistaken identity, deliberate disguise and random encounters in hotels. For the voyager, "there are too many wrong countries" and "already no one remembers you at home."

Despite the book's title, these poems are rarely autobiographical – though the tastes they reveal are intriguing – and they have few straightforward stories to tell. They are subtly humorous at one turn, sinister at another, heartbroken at the next. They puzzle over accidents, coincidences, and moments of passion, as they edge towards a sense of the world's curious strangeness, the complications of history and the encounters brought by the geography of migration.

Poems balance on the edge between concealment and revelation, between bemused fascination and tentative comprehension. Yet for all the disguises, the book offers glimpses of a distinctive and engaging sensibility involved with art, language and the nature of love. While Trinidad is scarcely mentioned, this is, if obliquely, the work of a poet trying to make sense of what it means to write in such an island society.